XL MACHINES!

BACKHOES

SETH KINGSTON

New York

Published in 2020 by The Rosen Publishing Group, Inc.
29 East 21st Street, New York, NY 10010

First Edition

Editor: Elizabeth Krajnik
Book Design: Michael Flynn

Photo Credits: Cover, pp. 1, 5, 17 Dmitry Kalinovsky/Shutterstock.com; series background (dirt) exopixel/Shutterstock.com; p. 7 Deep Desert Photography/Shutterstock.com; p. 9 JDziedzic/Shutterstock.com; p. 11 al7/Shutterstock.com; p. 13 Print Collector/Hulton Archive/Getty Images; p. 15 BCFC/Shutterstock.com; p. 19 SUPEE PURATO/Shutterstock.com; p. 21 easyshutter/Shutterstock.com; p. 22 Solcan Design/Shutterstock.com.

Cataloging-in-Publication Data

Names: Kingston, Seth.
Title: Backhoes / Seth Kingston.
Description: New York : PowerKids Press, 2020. | Series: XL machines! | Includes glossary and index.
Identifiers: ISBN 9781725311343(pbk.) | ISBN 9781725311367(library bound) | ISBN 9781725311350 (6pack)
Subjects: LCSH: Backhoes–Juvenile literature. | Excavating machinery–Juvenile literature.
Classification: LCC TA735.K56 2020 | DDC 629.225–dc23

Manufactured in the United States of America

CPSIA Compliance Information: Batch #CSPK19. For Further Information contact Rosen Publishing, New York, New York at 1-800-237-9932.

CONTENTS

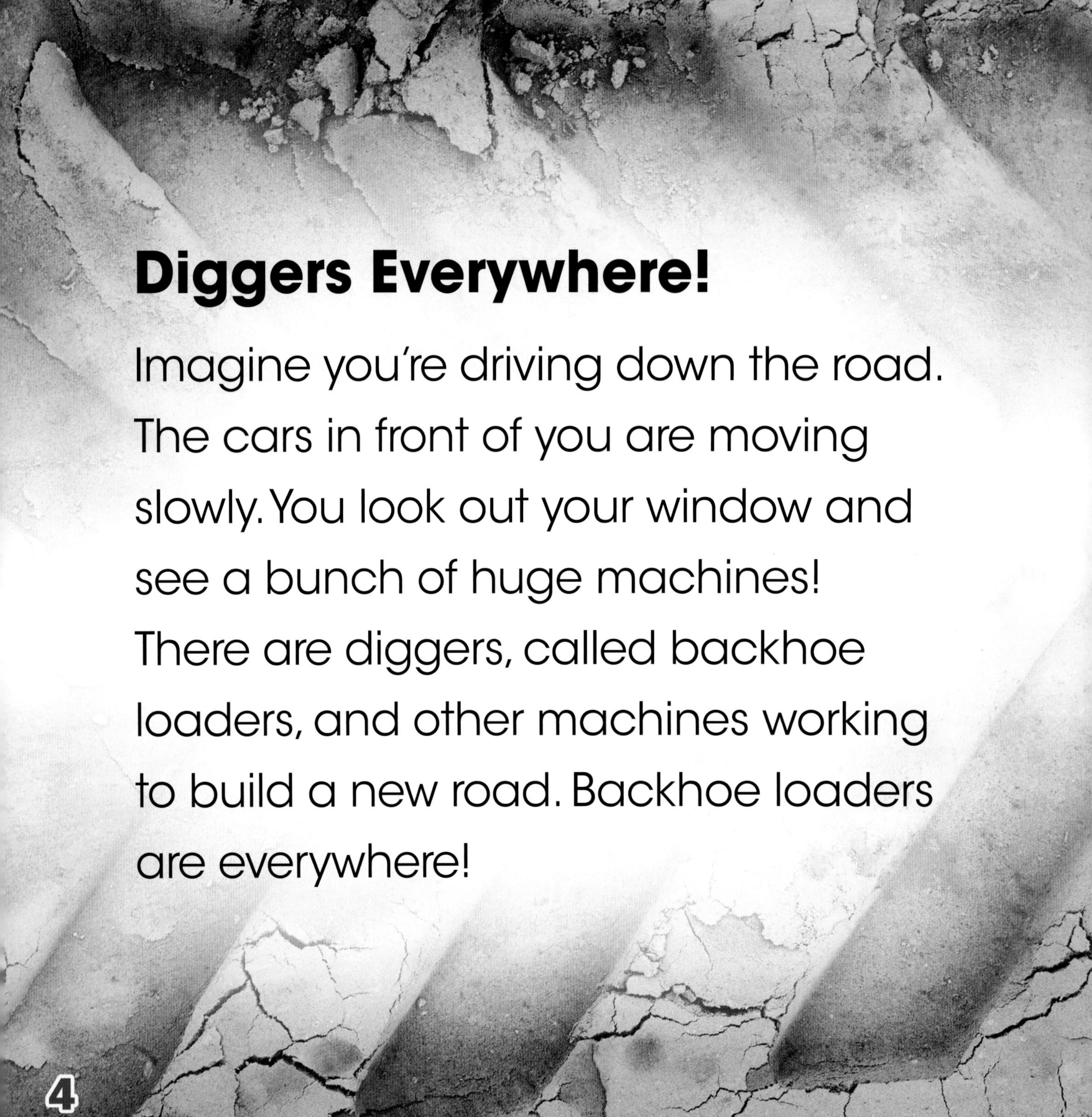

Diggers Everywhere!

Imagine you're driving down the road. The cars in front of you are moving slowly. You look out your window and see a bunch of huge machines! There are diggers, called backhoe loaders, and other machines working to build a new road. Backhoe loaders are everywhere!

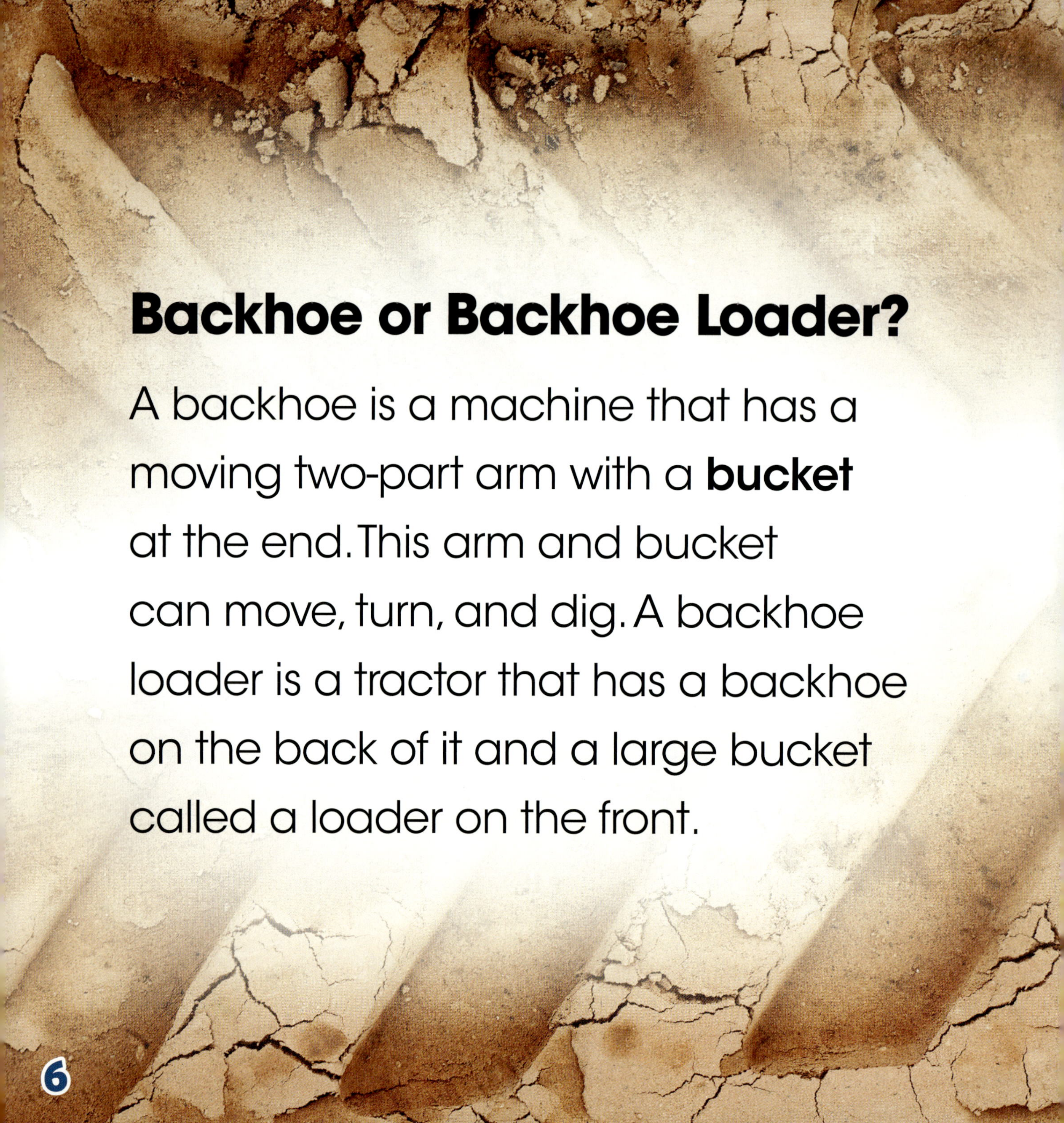

Backhoe or Backhoe Loader?

A backhoe is a machine that has a moving two-part arm with a **bucket** at the end. This arm and bucket can move, turn, and dig. A backhoe loader is a tractor that has a backhoe on the back of it and a large bucket called a loader on the front.

loader

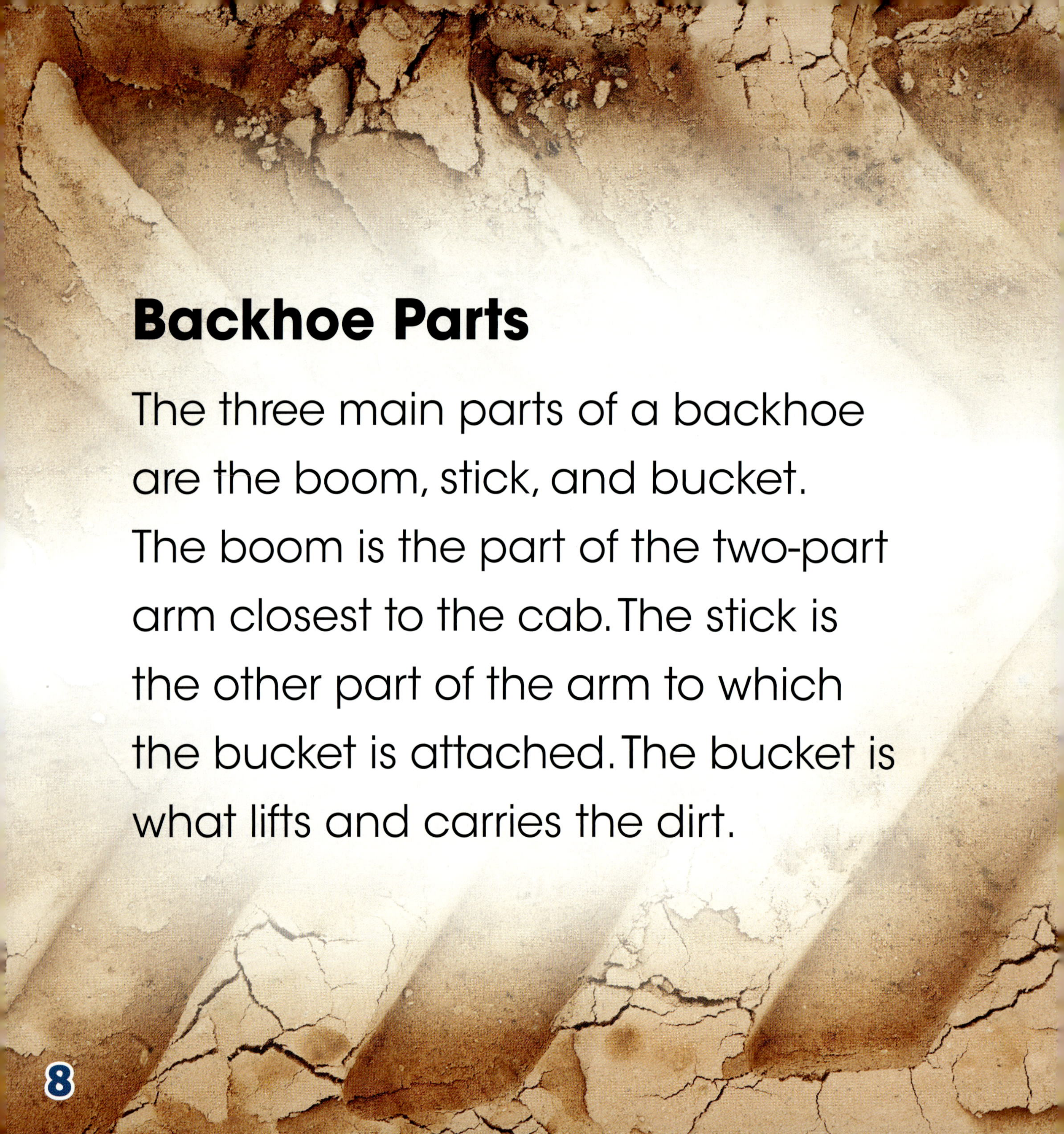

Backhoe Parts

The three main parts of a backhoe are the boom, stick, and bucket. The boom is the part of the two-part arm closest to the cab. The stick is the other part of the arm to which the bucket is attached. The bucket is what lifts and carries the dirt.

stick
boom
bucket

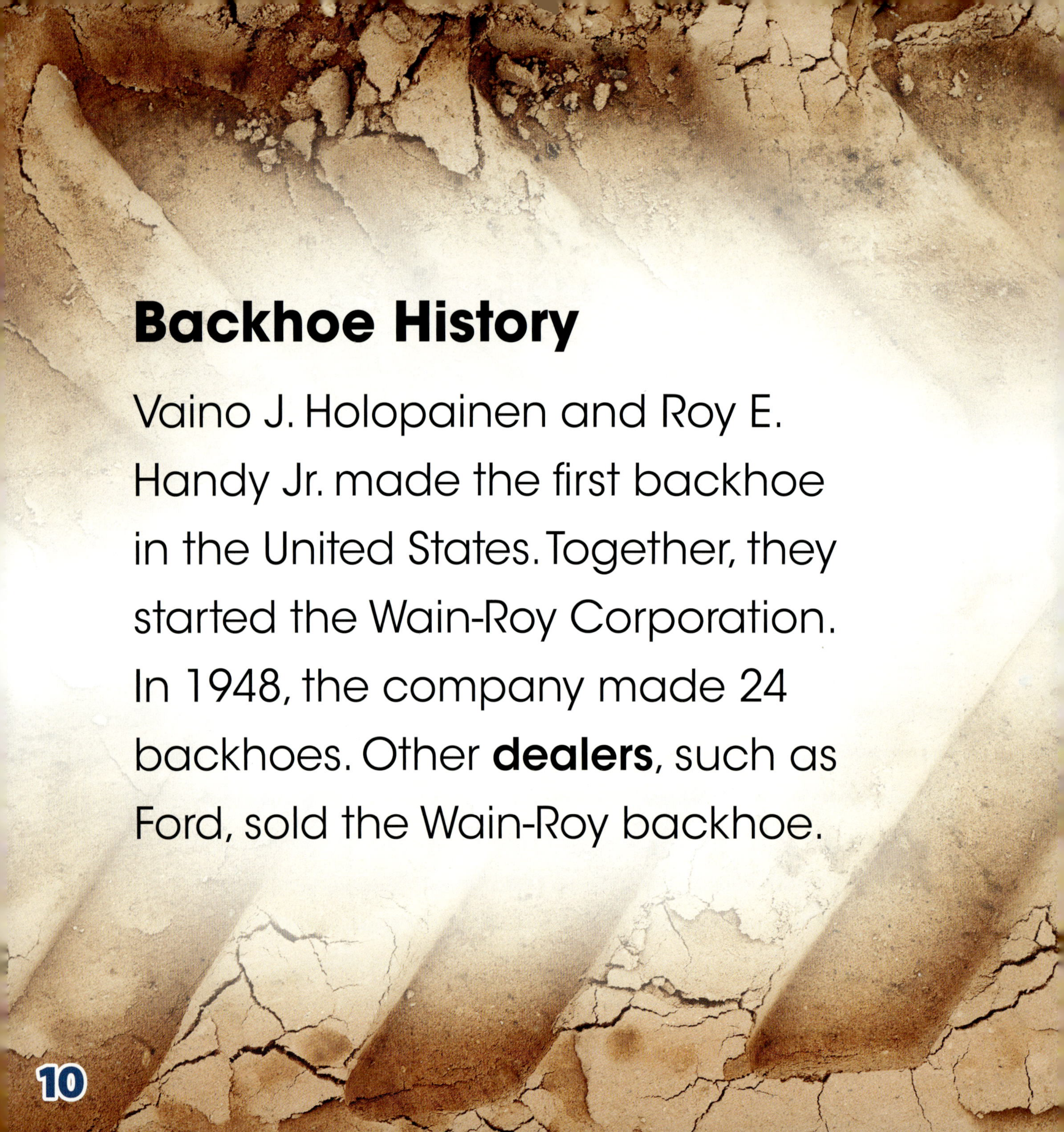

Backhoe History

Vaino J. Holopainen and Roy E. Handy Jr. made the first backhoe in the United States. Together, they started the Wain-Roy Corporation. In 1948, the company made 24 backhoes. Other **dealers**, such as Ford, sold the Wain-Roy backhoe.

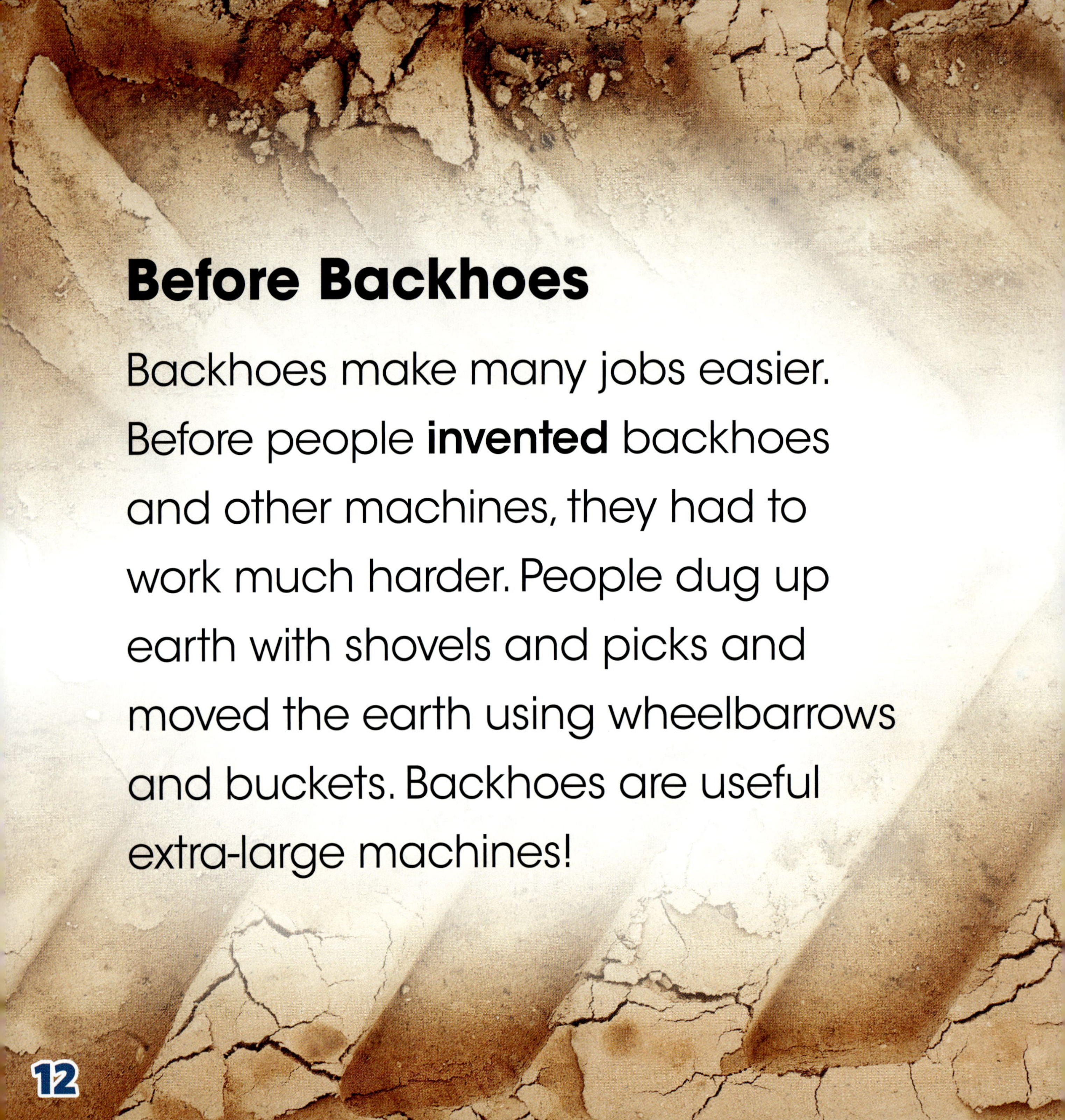

Before Backhoes

Backhoes make many jobs easier. Before people **invented** backhoes and other machines, they had to work much harder. People dug up earth with shovels and picks and moved the earth using wheelbarrows and buckets. Backhoes are useful extra-large machines!

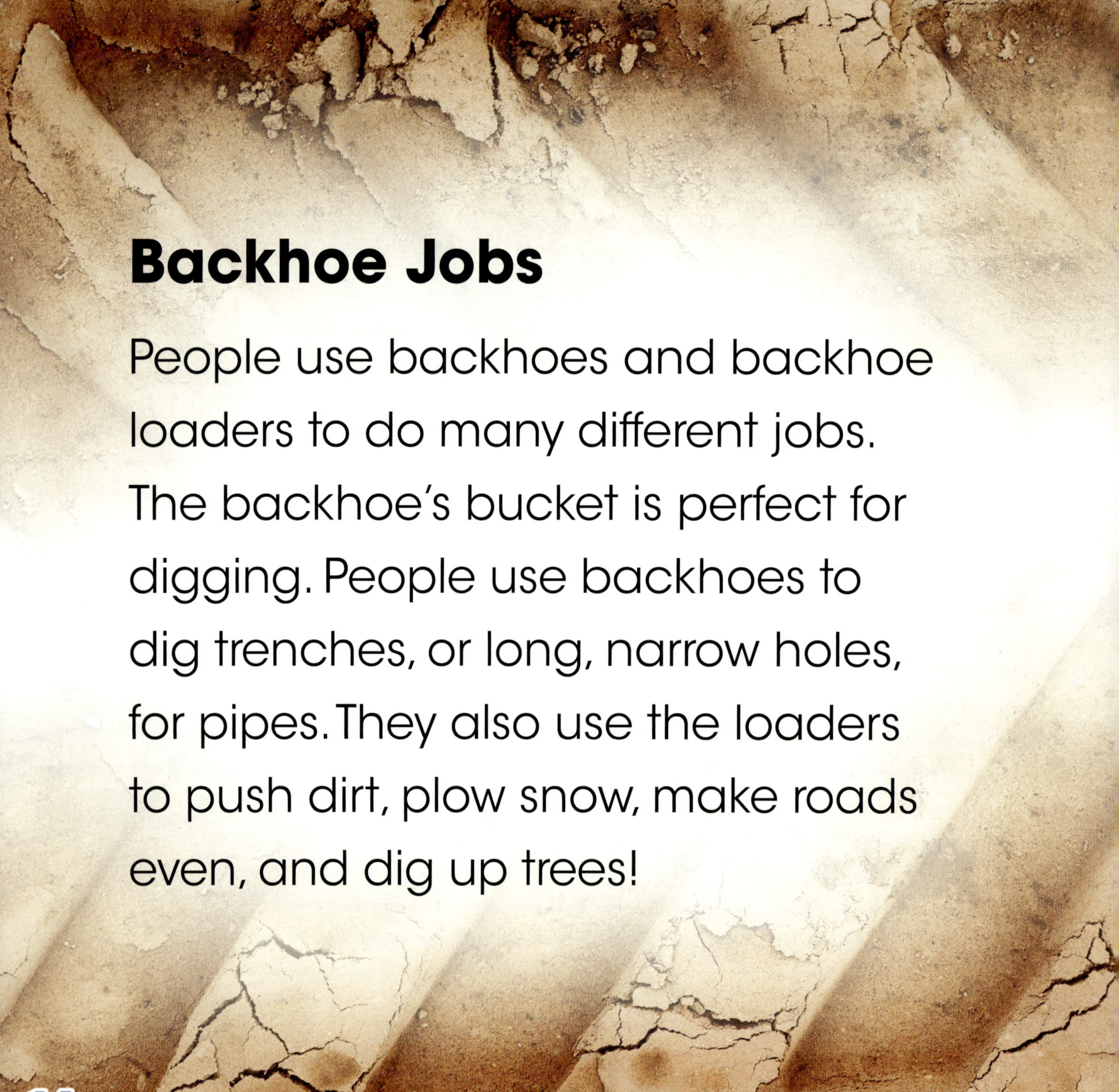

Backhoe Jobs

People use backhoes and backhoe loaders to do many different jobs. The backhoe's bucket is perfect for digging. People use backhoes to dig trenches, or long, narrow holes, for pipes. They also use the loaders to push dirt, plow snow, make roads even, and dig up trees!

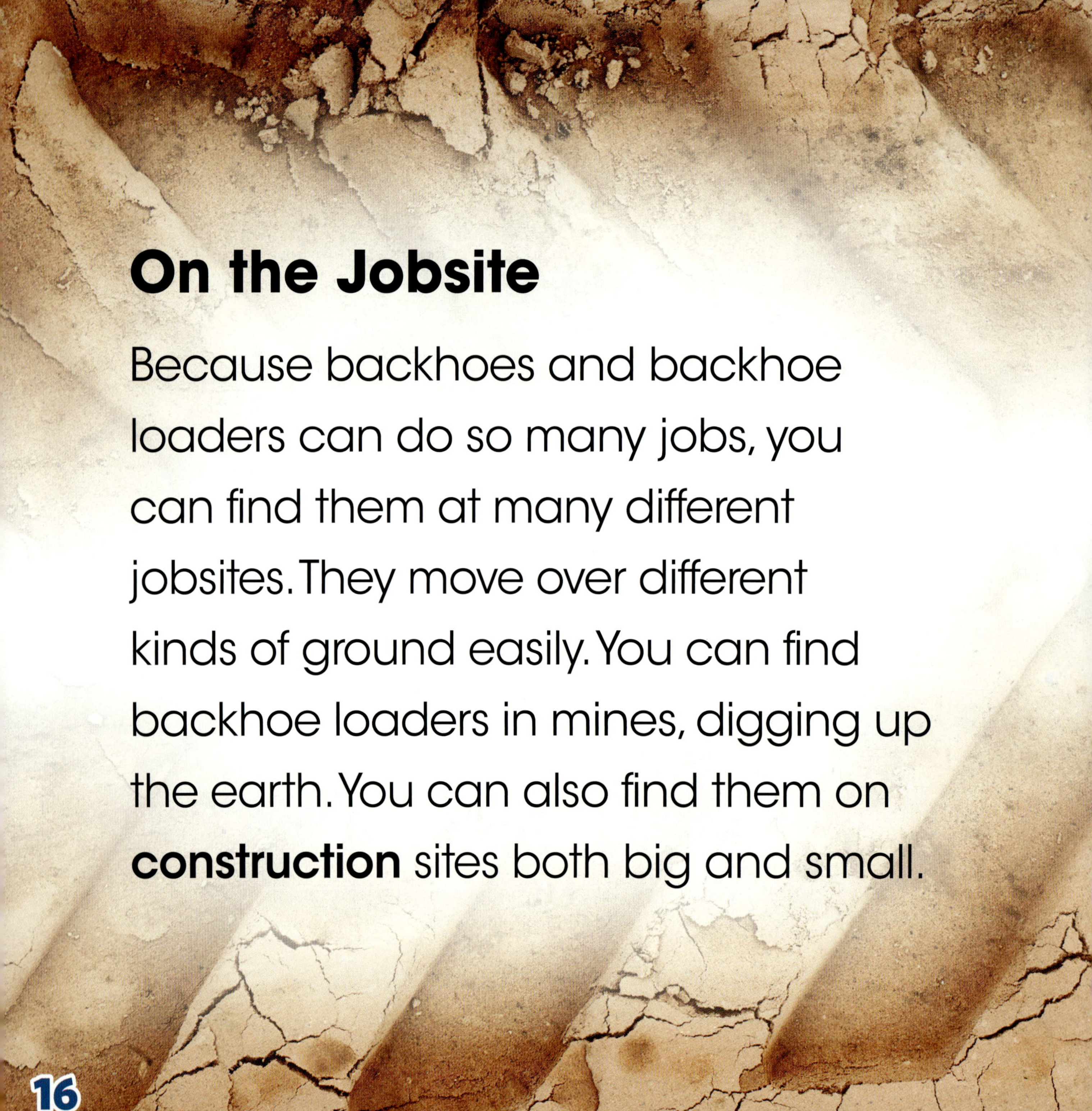

On the Jobsite

Because backhoes and backhoe loaders can do so many jobs, you can find them at many different jobsites. They move over different kinds of ground easily. You can find backhoe loaders in mines, digging up the earth. You can also find them on **construction** sites both big and small.

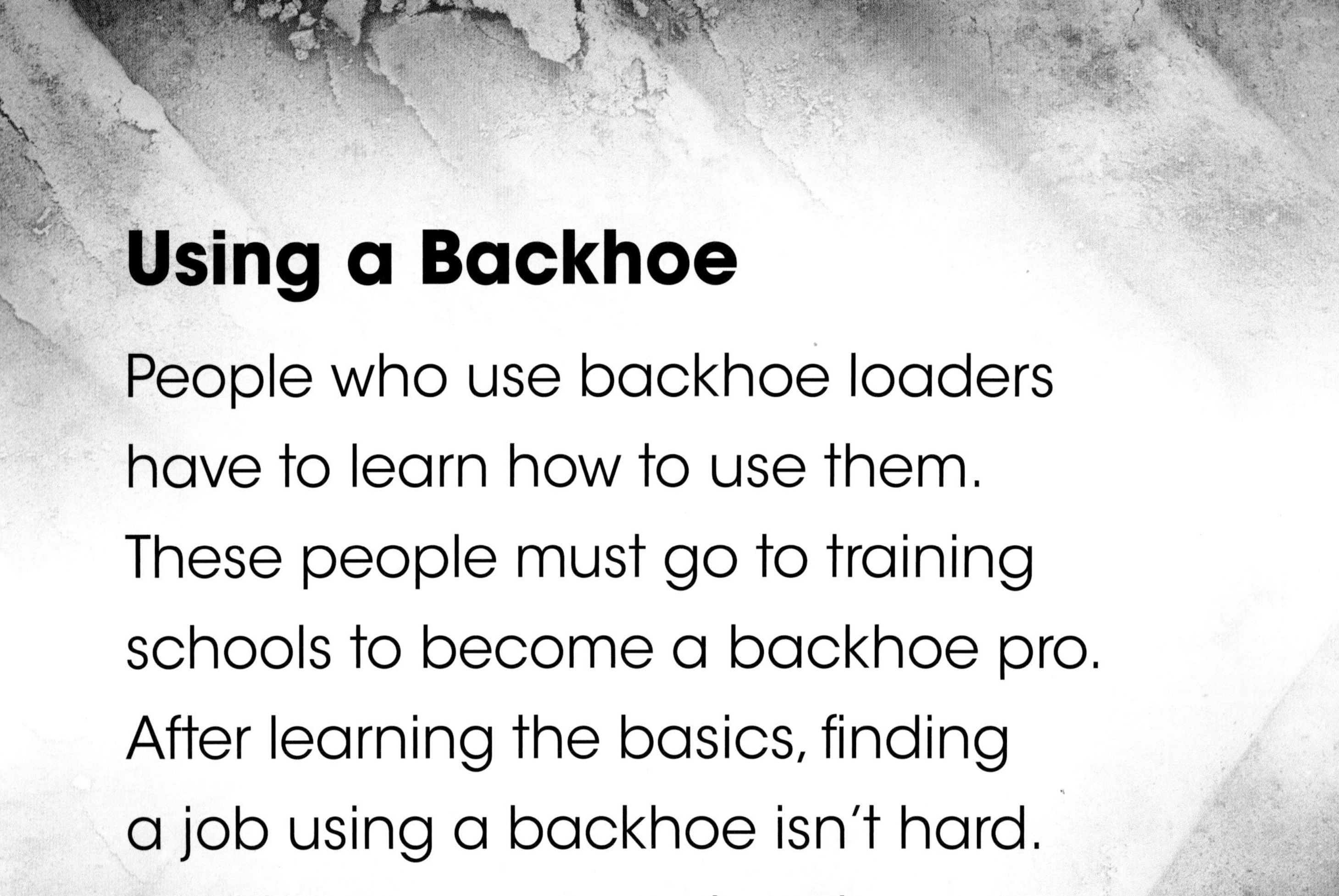

Using a Backhoe

People who use backhoe loaders have to learn how to use them. These people must go to training schools to become a backhoe pro. After learning the basics, finding a job using a backhoe isn't hard. Backhoes are everywhere!

Not a Backhoe Loader

An excavator is another kind of extra-large digger. Excavators have a backhoe, but they aren't backhoe loaders. They have a cab on a spinning base, which sits on top of tracks or wheels. Excavators can do many jobs, but not as many as a backhoe loader can!

Important Machines

Backhoes are important machines! Without them, many things wouldn't be possible. Some jobs would take many more people and even more hard work. These extra-large machines are commonly found on many different jobsites. Have you seen a backhoe?

GLOSSARY

bucket: A large container that may be part of a machine and is used for collecting, scooping, or carrying.

construction: Having to do with the act of building something.

dealer: A business that sells something, such as cars or other machines.

invent: To create or produce something useful for the first time.

INDEX

WEBSITES

Due to the changing nature of Internet links, PowerKids Press has developed an online list of websites related to the subject of this book. This site is updated regularly. Please use this link to access the list: www.powerkidslinks.com/xlm/backhoes